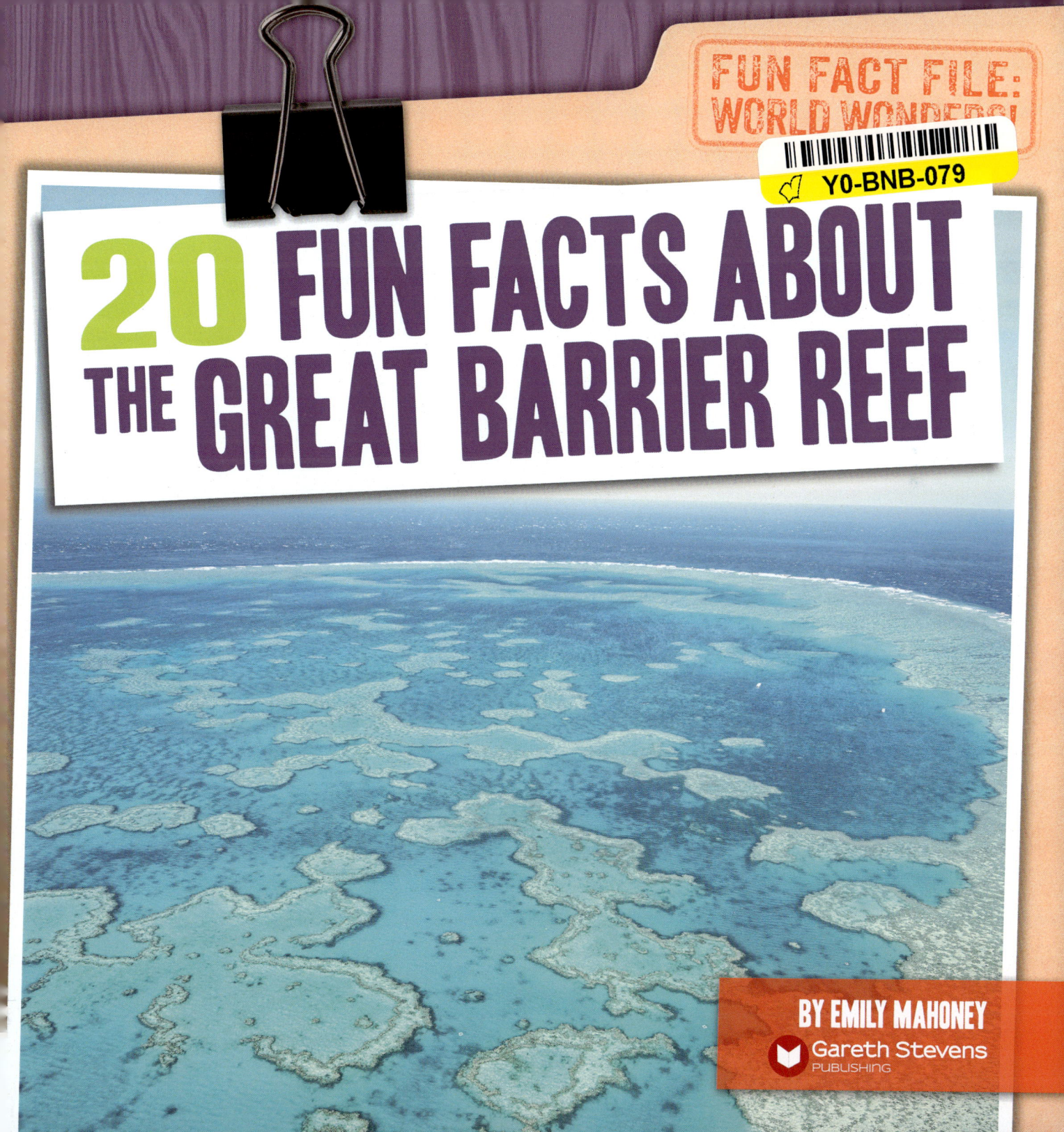

# 20 FUN FACTS ABOUT THE GREAT BARRIER REEF

Fun Fact File: World Wonders!

BY EMILY MAHONEY

Gareth Stevens
PUBLISHING

Please visit our website, www.garethstevens.com. For a free color catalog of all our high-quality books, call toll free 1-800-542-2595 or fax 1-877-542-2596.

Cataloging-in-Publication Data

Names: Mahoney, Emily.
Title: 20 fun facts about the great barrier reef / Emily Mahoney.
Description: New York : Gareth Stevens Publishing, 2020. | Series: Fun fact file: world wonders! | Includes glossary and index.
Identifiers: ISBN 9781538237748 (pbk.) | ISBN 9781538237762 (library bound) | ISBN 9781538237755 (6 pack)
Sbjects: LCSH: Coral reef ecology–Australia–Great Barrier Reef (Qld.)–Juvenile literature. | Great Barrier Reef (Qld.)–Juvenile literature.
Classification: LCC QE566.G7 M34 2020 | DDC 577.7'89–dc23

First Edition

Published in 2020 by
**Gareth Stevens Publishing**
111 East 14th Street, Suite 349
New York, NY 10003

Copyright © 2020 Gareth Stevens Publishing

Designer: Sarah Liddell
Editor: Kristen Nelson

Photo credits: Cover, p. 1 atiger/Shutterstock.com; file folder used throughout David Smart/Shutterstock.com; binder clip used throughout luckyraccoon/Shutterstock.com; wood grain background used throughout ARENA Creative/Shutterstock.com; pp. 5, 14, 16, 29 Brian Kinney/Shutterstock.com; p. 6 JC Photo/Shutterstock.com; p. 7 Universal History Archive/Contributor/Universal Images Group/Getty Images; p. 8 superjoseph/Shutterstock.com; p. 9 Serban Bogdan/Shutterstock.com; p. 10 Wagsy/Shutterstock.com; p. 11 Wayne0216/Shutterstock.com; p. 12 Trzęsacz/Wikimedia Commons; p. 13 Print Collector/Contributor/Hulton Archive/Getty Images; p. 15 JonMilnes/Shutterstock.com; p. 17 (clownfish) Oksana Golubeva/Shutterstock.com; p. 17 (surgeon fish) sirtravelalot/Shutterstock.com; p. 17 (butterfly fish) Vladislav Gajic/Shutterstock.com; p. 17 (parrot fish) J.S. Lamy/Shutterstock.com; p. 17 (grouper) Jacopo/Wikimedia Commons; p. 17 (coral trout) Rich Carey/Shutterstock.com; p. 18 Claudio Soldi/Shutterstock.com; p. 19 lisnic/Shutterstock.com; p. 20 Ian Scott/Shutterstock.com; p. 21 Auscape/Contributor/Universal Images Group/Getty Images; p. 22 ChameleonsEye/Shutterstock.com; p. 23 EpochCatcher/Shutterstock.com; p. 24 The Sydney Morning Herald/Contributor/Fairfax Media/Getty Images; p. 25 Tunatura/Shutterstock.com; p. 26 Richard Whitcombe/Shutterstock.com; p. 27 GREG WOOD/Staff/AFP/Getty Images.

All rights reserved. No part of this book may be reproduced in any form without permission in writing from the publisher, except by a reviewer.

Printed in the United States of America

CPSIA compliance information: Batch #CS19GS: For further information contact Gareth Stevens, New York, New York at 1-800-542-2595.

# CONTENTS

A Great Coral Reef . . . . . . . . . . . . . . . . . . . . . . . . . . . . . . . 4
Location and Size. . . . . . . . . . . . . . . . . . . . . . . . . . . . . . . . 6
Reef Formation. . . . . . . . . . . . . . . . . . . . . . . . . . . . . . . . . 10
Exploring the Reef . . . . . . . . . . . . . . . . . . . . . . . . . . . . . 12
Waters of the Reef . . . . . . . . . . . . . . . . . . . . . . . . . . . . . 14
Reef Species . . . . . . . . . . . . . . . . . . . . . . . . . . . . . . . . . . 16
Visiting the Reef . . . . . . . . . . . . . . . . . . . . . . . . . . . . . . . 22
Reef Conservation . . . . . . . . . . . . . . . . . . . . . . . . . . . . . 26
A Beautiful Place . . . . . . . . . . . . . . . . . . . . . . . . . . . . . . 28
Glossary . . . . . . . . . . . . . . . . . . . . . . . . . . . . . . . . . . . . . 30
For More Information . . . . . . . . . . . . . . . . . . . . . . . . . . 31
Index . . . . . . . . . . . . . . . . . . . . . . . . . . . . . . . . . . . . . . . 32

Words in the glossary appear in **bold** type the first time they are used in the text.

# A GREAT CORAL REEF

The Great Barrier Reef amazes everyone who has the chance to see it. Many kinds of coral, fish, sea turtles, and sharks are just some of the creatures that call this beautiful area home!

The Great Barrier Reef is often called one of the seven natural wonders of the world. This enormous wonder is found in the Pacific Ocean, off the northeast coast of Australia. It's so big, that visitors can explore for several days—and still not see all of it!

Much of the reef can be seen above the water, but there's so much life underwater, too!

# LOCATION AND SIZE

**FUN FACT: 1**

**THE GREAT BARRIER REEF IS ABOUT HALF THE SIZE OF THE STATE OF TEXAS!**

It's made up of thousands of individual reefs. It stretches over 1,400 miles (2,253 km). Its area is about 135,000 square miles (349,648 sq km).

The Great Barrier Reef is the largest and longest reef complex on Earth.

The Great Barrier Reef can be seen in the upper half of this picture, which was taken by a **satellite** in space.

# FUN FACT: 2

## THE GREAT BARRIER REEF CAN BE SEEN FROM SPACE.

That means astronauts can see it! Reefs are easy to see from space because the light blue color of the shallow water around them **contrasts** with the dark blue color of deeper water.

## FUN FACT: 3

### A PERSON COULD SWIM TO THE GREAT BARRIER REEF—BUT IT WOULD BE REALLY FAR!

The reef is located anywhere from 10 to 100 miles (16 to 160 km) off the coast of Australia. Most people take a boat to parts of the Great Barrier Reef.

The warm temperature of the water in this part of the ocean makes it a great place for the reef to grow.

# WHERE IS THE GREAT BARRIER REEF?

GREAT BARRIER REEF

AUSTRALIA

This map shows how far the Great Barrier Reef stretches along Australia's coast.

# REEF FORMATION

**FUN FACT: 4**

## THE GREAT BARRIER REEF IS ABOUT 500,000 YEARS OLD.

It's changed a lot over time, though! The form of the reef today is about 6,000 to 8,000 years old. The reef's makeup can vary based on the sea level, which changes over time.

Corals are very small. This photograph shows many coral skeletons joined together.

FUN FACT: 5

## THE GREAT BARRIER REEF IS MADE OF ANIMALS.

Corals are animals! The reef is made up of many **species** of both living coral colonies and coral that died long ago. Many species have a hard skeleton that's left behind when they die. These remains make up most of the reef.

# EXPLORING THE REEF

**FUN FACT: 6**

**EUROPEAN EXPLORERS DIDN'T SPOT THE GREAT BARRIER REEF UNTIL THE MID-1700S!**

On one notable early journey, James Cook spent a few months sailing near the reef in 1770. He didn't know it was there until his ship ran into it!

Cook wasn't trying to find or explore the reef. In fact, he was studying the planet Venus from his ship!

**FUN FACT: 7**

## PASSAGES THROUGH THE REEF ARE NAMED FOR THE PEOPLE WHO FOUND THEM.

For example, Cook's Passage is named for James Cook, and Flinders Passage is named for Matthew Flinders. As more people traveled near Australia, ways around and through the reef were discovered!

# WATERS OF THE REEF

**FUN FACT: 8**

**THE SURFACE TEMPERATURE OF THE WATER RANGES FROM 70° TO 100°F (21° TO 38°C).**

The water temperature of the Great Barrier Reef doesn't change much from season to season, which makes it perfect for coral growth. The warm water is also comfortable for animals that live on the reef, as well as for divers!

The Great Barrier Reef is one of the top **scuba diving** locations in the world because of how well divers can see in the clear water.

## FUN FACT: 9

### FROM THE WATER'S SURFACE, YOU CAN SEE THE REEF TO A DEPTH OF ABOUT 100 FEET (30 M)!

This might not always be the case, however. There's great concern about the future water **quality** around the reef. The Australian government has begun working to reduce pollution that flows into the water, particularly from farming.

# REEF SPECIES

**FUN FACT: 10**

**ABOUT 10 PERCENT OF ALL THE KINDS OF FISH ON EARTH LIVE WITHIN THE GREAT BARRIER REEF!**

There are more than 1,500 species of fish that live on the reef. Since there are many fish from each species, that means the number of actual fish living here is quite high!

# FISH ON THE REEF

**CLOWN FISH**

**SURGEON FISH**

**BUTTERFLY FISH**

**PARROT FISH**

**GROUPER**

**CORAL TROUT**

You'll have the chance to see many colorful fish if you go scuba diving at the Great Barrier Reef!

## FUN FACT: 11

### THIRTY SPECIES OF DOLPHINS, WHALES, AND PORPOISES HAVE BEEN SPOTTED AROUND THE GREAT BARRIER REEF.

Whales, dolphins, and porpoises are all **mammals**. Some species you may see at the reef are orcas (killer whales), sperm whales, humpback whales, bottlenose dolphins, and spinner dolphins!

HUMPBACK WHALE

## FUN FACT: 12

## SIX OF THE WORLD'S SEVEN SEA TURTLE SPECIES MAY BE SPOTTED ON THE REEF.

The most commonly seen species are green turtles and loggerhead turtles. Others, such as olive ridley turtles and leatherback turtles, also live there but aren't seen as often.

Whitetip reef sharks rest in reef caves during the day. Sometimes many sharks stay in a cave together stacked on top of one another!

FUN FACT: 13

## THE WHITETIP REEF SHARK IS THE SHARK MOST COMMONLY SEEN ON THE REEF.

Sharks aren't as common as fish, whales, or sea turtles, but you might still see one near the reef! Some other shark species you may see are blacktip reef sharks and grey reef whalers.

## SOME ANIMALS THAT LIVE AROUND THE GREAT BARRIER REEF ARE PROTECTED.

The dugong, or sea cow, is just one animal that could be at risk of dying out. Other protected animals on the Great Barrier Reef are sea snakes, sea dragons, and sea turtles.

That means the animals' population might be very low or their future survival might be in danger from human activities. These species are watched and sometimes specially cared for by government groups.

21

# VISITING THE REEF

**FUN FACT: 15**

**THE GREAT BARRIER REEF HAS ABOUT 2 MILLION VISITORS EACH YEAR.**

The reef is one of the seven natural wonders of the world! Most people visit in June through October because there isn't a lot of rain during those months and the water is very clear.

More than 120 people died when the SS *Yongala* sank. The wreck went undiscovered for almost 50 years!

FUN FACT: 16

## THERE ARE ABOUT 800 SHIPWRECKS ON THE REEF!

You can explore the marine life that's taken over some of these wrecks and also learn a lot about the history of the ships. One of the most popular wrecks—the SS *Yongala*—sank in a **cyclone** in 1911.

23

## FUN FACT: 17

### VISITORS CAN SEE DEEP UNDERWATER WITHOUT GETTING WET!

Glass-bottom boat tours allow you to experience the reef in a whole new way. Tours using boats with clear bottoms started during the 1930s! Today, many people like to see the reef this way.

Scuba diving is another great way to see the wildlife of the Great Barrier Reef. You'll need special training before you go, though.

## FUN FACT: 18

### YOU CAN TAKE PICTURES UNDERWATER AT THE GREAT BARRIER REEF!

You can use a special underwater camera when snorkeling, or swimming underwater with a special mask and tube called a snorkel to help you breathe. Snorkeling is a great way to see sea turtles, rays, and many fish.

# REEF CONSERVATION

**FUN FACT: 19**

## THE GREAT BARRIER REEF IS IN DANGER.

Pollution and **runoff** can harm the reef's water and wildlife. Runoff may be one reason for increases in the population of crown-of-thorns starfish. The **nutrients** in runoff cause overgrowth of phytoplankton, tiny sea animals the starfish larvae eat.

Adult crown-of-thorns starfish eat the corals that make up the reef!

Many conservation groups work to keep the reef safe. Conservation is the care of the natural world.

FUN FACT: 20

## VISITORS ARE HELPING SAVE THE GREAT BARRIER REEF!

Many human activities are adding to climate change, or the slow warming of Earth and its waters, which hurts the reef **ecosystem**. But, those who visit the Great Barrier Reef pay a "reef tax." This money goes toward everyday efforts to keep the reef ecosystem healthy and clean.

# A BEAUTIFUL PLACE

The Great Barrier Reef is known worldwide as a fantastic wonder. However, this world wonder needs help to be kept safe and clean so the coral and other animals living there can survive and grow.

By making sure others know about the dangers facing the Great Barrier Reef and taking action together, we can make sure this ecosystem will be around for years to come! As more people see the beauty of the Great Barrier Reef, more people will want to save it!

The reef ecosystem is important because it gives many animals homes, food, and places to have their babies.

# GLOSSARY

**contrast:** to be different in an obvious way

**cyclone:** a large and powerful storm with very high winds

**ecosystem:** all living and nonliving things in an area

**mammal:** a warm-blooded animal that has a backbone and hair, breathes air, and feeds milk to its young

**nutrient:** something a living thing needs to grow and stay alive

**quality:** how good or bad something is

**runoff:** water from rain or snow that flows over land into a body of water. It often carries harmful matter.

**satellite:** an object that circles Earth in order to collect and send information or aid in communication

**scuba diving:** a sport in which someone swims underwater using an air tank and a special breathing machine

**species:** a group of plants or animals that are all of the same kind

# FOR MORE INFORMATION

## BOOKS

Medina, Nico. *Where Is the Great Barrier Reef?* New York, NY: Grosset & Dunlap, 2016.

Simon, Seymour. *Coral Reefs.* New York, NY: Harper Collins, 2013.

## WEBSITES

**Fun Facts About the Great Barrier Reef**
www.fun-facts.org.uk/wonders_of_world/great-barrier-reef.htm
Fun facts and pictures of the reef are easy to access on this site.

**Great Barrier Reef Facts (for Kids)**
greatbarrierreef.com.au/information/for-kids/
Find information and videos about the Great Barrier Reef here.

**Publisher's note to educators and parents:** Our editors have carefully reviewed these websites to ensure that they are suitable for students. Many websites change frequently, however, and we cannot guarantee that a site's future contents will continue to meet our high standards of quality and educational value. Be advised that students should be closely supervised whenever they access the internet.

# INDEX

age 10

Australia 4, 8, 9, 13

boats 8, 24

climate change 27

conservation groups 27

Cook, James 12, 13

coral 4, 11, 14, 26, 28

crown-of-thorns starfish 26

divers 14, 15

dolphins 18

dugongs 21

ecosystem 27, 28, 29

explorers 12

fish 4, 16, 17, 20, 25

formation 10

Pacific Ocean 4

passages 13

pollution 15, 26

porpoises 18

protected animals 21

reef tax 27

runoff 26

scuba diving 15, 17, 25

sea turtles 4, 19, 20, 21, 25

sharks 4, 20

shipwrecks 23

size 6

snorkeling 25

space 7

SS *Yongala* 23

temperature 8, 14

underwater cameras 25

visitors 4, 22, 24, 27

water quality 15

whales 18, 20